# YOUR KNOWLEDGE HAS VALUE

# Reducing Verbal Stereotypy in a Student with Autism Spectrum Disorder

Naff Kennedy Aineya

**Bibliographic information published by the German National Library:**

The German National Library lists this publication in the National Bibliography; detailed bibliographic data are available on the Internet at http://dnb.dnb.de.

ISBN: 9783346775108
This book is also available as an ebook.

© GRIN Publishing GmbH
Nymphenburger Straße 86
80636 München

Print and binding: Books on Demand GmbH, Norderstedt, Germany
Printed on acid-free paper from responsible sources.

The present work has been carefully prepared. Nevertheless, authors and publishers do not incur liability for the correctness of information, notes, links and advice as well as any printing errors.

GRIN web shop: https://www.grin.com/document/1302515

**Reducing Verbal Stereotypy in a Student with Autism Condition (ASD)**


A Literature Review

Author: Naff Kennedy Aineya

BBA Accounting

University of Eastern Africa, Baraton

Date Modified: Monday, November 16, 2022

**Reducing Verbal Stereotypy in a Student with Autism Condition (ASD)**

A student with autism spectrum disorder has speaking, learning, and socialization problems and consistently involve in repetitive habits (Posar et al., 2019). Studies show adequate interventions for the students are lacking, but development is made in learning, socialization, adaptive and intellectual skills (Ahearn et al., 2007). Stereotyping is a core symptom referred to repetitive behaviorist and topographic invariant. Echolalia, contextual verbs, and vocalization are stereotypies controlled by automated positive reinforcement. The condition hinders learning if the behavior consumes the student's daily activities and limits participation in activities, such as vocation, leisure, and skills in academic settings (Esposito et al., 2021). Therefore, treating stereotypies decreases the stigmatization of a student with ASD.

Ahearn et al. (2007) also confirm that autism condition regards impairment in speaking, listening, socialization, and communication, indicated by restrictive and repetitive stereotyped behavior. It is critical to detect the situation early and begin targeted treatment (Sălăgean & Stan, 2020). Memari et al. (2015) suggest that children with vocal stereotypy condition face challenges concerning age group games and fail to develop social relationships (Lanovaz et al., 2011). Esposito et al. (2021) examined stereotypy habits shown by a seven-year child with autism and controlled by automatic reinforcement under stimulus conditions. Using discriminative training method. The discriminative training involves matching a green card (SD) with free access to vocal stereotypy and a red card (SD-absent) with interruption of stereotypy and vocal redirection (Dunlop, 2012). Kahveci & Bulut (2019) concentrated on the non-aversive vocal and speaking teaching method with reinforcement protocols to enhance the frequency of communication attempts in students with ASD. Vocal stereotypy is now understood to have the potential for learning development, although they have delayed social consequences. Stereotypy's underlying causes are unknown, and many researchers and scientists have done studies on appropriate intervention, but the result has produced varied results (Dunlop, 2012). The paper expounds on the early features of autism condition (ASD) and frequencies of Involvement in daily games, plays, and physical activities. Stimulus control using red card/green card, vocal self-stimulation, and the effect of multiple interventions for decreasing speaking stereotypy in a child (student) with autism.

**Early Features of Autism Condition (ASD)**

Autism concerns speaking, socialization, and communication impairment, indicated by restrictive and repetitive stereotyped behavior. It is critical to detect the situation early and begin targeted treatment. Posar et al. (2019) report on the first signs, age, and mode of the exhibition in children with autism condition. He also classified the symptoms at the beginning according to relationship, language, and social interaction. It considered three modes of presentation: regression of development, stagnation, and delay.

Posar et al. (2019) suggest that early symptoms are seen at seven and twelve months and between thirteen to twenty-four months. However, there were no considerable differences in the age at onset concerning etiopathogenesis, intelligence quotient levels, and early-onset epilepsy (Posar et al., 2019). Delay in spoken language is a common symptom, creating the need for diagnosis and initial medication (Posar et al., 2019). There were many eating problems and cases of development stagnation and delays (Posar et al., 2019). Language problems were few and cases of regression, while movement and physical activities were many in some cases and with little delays.

**Frequencies of Involvement in Daily Games, Plays, and Physical Activities**

Researchers suggest that a child with a vocal stereotypy condition faces challenges concerning peer games and fails to develop a social relationships (Memari et al., 2015). He recommends that students should frequently involve in leisure activities, such as hobbies, social activities, and sports (Memari et al., 2015). However, students with autism spectrum conditions take their passive games and are not commonly involved in group or peer activities. Investigation of the daily physical activity using 83 children, including 31 girls and 52 boys aged 6 to 15, provides evidence of stagnation in development and speaking stereotype in students with autism. Memari et al. (2015) concluded that twelve percent of the students were physically active but were involved in solidary games rather than social games (Memari et al. (2015). Household income, gender, and family structures were confirmed to impact physical activity scores (Memari et al. (2015). His study confirms lower physical activities and participation in peer play with a student with an autism condition are very connected with socio-demographic variables. Lack of opportunities and financial burden was leading to barriers to physical activities.

**Stimulus Control Using Red card/Green Card**

Esposito et al. (2021) examined stereotypy habits shown by a seven-year child with autism condition and controlled by automatic reinforcement supported by stimulus manipulation or discrimination method. The discrimination involves training and matching a green card (SD with free access to speaking stereotypy) and a red card (with no SD, the stereotypy is interrupted, and the music sound is redirected). After the discrimination session, the child/student speaks stereotypically with the red card rather than the green card, indicating the ability to select (Esposito et al., 2021). The red card latency period was more extended than the green card condition

(Esposito et al., 2021). The study proves that stimulus control intervention reduces vocal stereotypy in students with autism condition (ASD).

Studies on the impact of consequential and antecedent interventions, including visual cue cards and trade-in opportunities, indicate that treatment packages effectively reduce vocal stereotypy in school settings (Dunlop, 2012). The study found that reinforcement contingencies can maintain stereotypy. Behavioral research suggests people with autism cannot participate in social and environmental cues, and stereotypy further reduces the student's ability to follow instructions in the learning environment (Dunlop, 2012). Stereotypy may interfere not only with skills acquisition but with peer behaviors. Therefore interventions that teach the student how to manage autism and what they can or cannot do are beneficial.

**Nonlinguistic Contingent Responses, Imitation, and Linguistic Contingent Responses**

Kahveci & Bulut (2019) put up three groups for reducing speaking stereotypy in children with autism. The first class is called "nonlinguistic contingent response." The first group can be to acknowledge student behavior through imitation (Kahveci & Bulut, 2019). The imitation is expected to reduce the student's vocalizations while engaging in the favorite activity. The second group is called "Linguistic Contingent Responses." The second group involves directives and comments about the choices of the children's toys inside the research focus (Kahveci & Bulut, 2019). The last group is called "Linguistic Contingent Responses to the Child's Communication Act." the responses add language and communication to the student's actions (Kahveci & Bulut, 2019). These structured three-class responses are considered a non-aversive communication teaching technique (Esposito et al., 2021). The advantage of the technique is that it avoids the

4

condition, person, or behavior that triggers outbursts and improves the quality of life with positive behavioral support.

The discrimination training reinforces target behaviors in the presence of stimuli as they expect the student with ASD to behave appropriately in the presence of incentives and the absence of reinforcement (Esposito et al., 2021). The discriminative stimuli treatment and control method is used to teach children with ASD to adapt proper responses in academic, social, communication, vocational, and self-care skill. Esposito et al. (2021) found that a red/green card can control stereotypy. Extra stereotyping occurs when a green card is used than when a red card is used because of discriminatory catalyst intervention, causing a decrease of the stereotypy when the red card is used.

Kahveci & Bulut's (2019) research produces promising results in reducing repetitive vocalizations behavior in a child with ASD. The student-anticipated communication acts were reshaped to increase communicative acts (Kahveci & Bulut, 2019). At the beginning of the first intervention, the student frequency values were fewer than five; at the end, the frequency values increased to 25. A similar result was gathered in the second and third interventions (Kahveci & Bulut, 2019). The short-term outcome collected is used to predict long-term positive impacts and might help increase academic achievement and reduce school dropout in students with autism (Kahveci & Bulut, 2019). In the baseline sessions, the student had a negative mood and played alone without sharing toys (Any playing material). In the intervention phase, the student showed positive emotions, pleasure, a smiling face, eye contact, and diminishing repetitive vocalization. Students under OBS treatment performed better in communication and showed decreasing speaking stereotypes according to TAU (treatment-as-usual).

In functionality stereotypy, a positive reinforcement contingency can maintain motor and vocal stereotypy for access to attention because the main challenge is to sustain attention in academics, communication, and when playing with peers (Esposito et al., 2021). The echolalia repetitive behavior is reinforced by stimulation generated by the behavior and supported by the sensory actions it produces, and repetitive speaking can be supported by communication consequences (Esposito et al., 2021). Some studies use mild punishment in behavioral interventions to treat a student with ASD. Esposito et al. (2021) studies show a target habit interruption and controlling it by proper vocalization lowers speaking stereotypy in four treatments with an autistic child. The habit interruption may be replaced by questions regarding communication rules, such as how to request an item.

Socialization and adaptive habits are seen as impairments for those diagnosed with speaking stereotypy, and these habits might interfere with learning conditions. Kahveci & Bulut (2019) suggest response interruption and redirection coupled with differential treatment for undesired behaviors (RIRD + DRI) to strengthen proper vocalization. Positive behavior support (PBS) techniques explain the argument behind undesired habits (Kahveci & Bulut, 2019). The perspective can be used to consider vocal stereotypy as a speaking habit shaped by PBS. A teaching replacement skill (TRS) technique can replace inappropriate communication skills (Kahveci & Bulut, 2019). Teaching can shape speaking stereotypy in children diagnosed with autism using effective, such as mutual emotion sharing.

**Vocal Self-Stimulation**

A speaking stereotypy can interfere with the hearing process, learning, and expected social habits. Speaking self-stimulation is identified by repeating meaningless and noncontextual verbs.

6

Sălăgean & Stan (2020) examined the effects of restricting access to cartoons and interventions on speaking self-stimulation in a six-year child diagnosed with autism. His findings show that restricting access to comics and DRO-based interventions reduced vocal stereotypies (Sălăgean & Stan, 2020). Differential treatment method (DRO) reduces undesirable habits in ASD. It is a non-punitive procedure where reinforcers strengthen the response to alternative activity, encouraging adaptive behavior (Sălăgean & Stan, 2020).

ASD is characterized by limited communication, stereotypical behaviors, and deficient social interactions. Similarly, the frequency of vocal stereotypy concerns many parents and teachers because of the effect on social interaction and learning (Sălăgean & Stan, 2020). However, there is limited research on treating speaking-self stimulation because of the automatic reinforcement functions of the habits. Teachers often exclude a student with ASD from their classes, making it ineffective to find solutions to reduce these behaviors, facilitate better interaction between children, help them become receptive to a student with ASD, and improve learning (Sălăgean & Stan, 2020).

Sălăgean & Stan (2020) suggested that a student with ASD uses media differently from a normal student, that place the student at risk for a negative outcome, including cognitive, physiologic, emotional, social, and legal problems. The student has a strong preference for cartoons and media ads, a pattern correlated with the behavioral manifestation of ASD. Sălăgean & Stan (2020) finds that reinforcement with role-play game is a significant predictor of oppositional behavior in a student with ASD. The study found that ASD students prefer media with features for younger audiences and often imitate cartoons with observable benefits (Sălăgean & Stan, 2020).

Examining the frequency of vocal self-stimulation involves three stereotypical behaviors measured in one-on-one therapy and school settings (Sălăgean & Stan, 2020). Motor stereotype, vocal stereotypy, and combined motor and vocal stereotypy. The researcher calculated hourly rates and gathered information each time the student involves in the speaking stereotypy (Sălăgean & Stan, 2020).

The speaking (Vocal) self-stimulation occurs more consistently compared to motor stereotypy. It is more common in the school context than in the therapy center. Following the observation, Sălăgean & Stan (2020) finalized that watching comics could treat speaking self-stimulation in children. The results are interventions based on control access to cartoons and DRO. The children involved in speaking self-stimulation at approximately 25.99% intervals (Sălăgean & Stan, 2020). DRO interventions were also implemented two weeks after: the percentage of speaking self-stimulation happed below baseline estimates, showing a reducing trend (Sălăgean & Stan, 2020). The approximate intervals were 14.08%. When the baseline estimate was retested, the student's speaking self-stimulation was reduced to 10.83%. The ABAB reversal design confirms the intervention result (Sălăgean & Stan, 2020). The student vocal self-stimulation intervals decrease with intervention in the first phase, increase without intervention in the second phase, and decrease with the second intervention.

**Effect of Multiple Interventions for Reducing Speaking Stereotypy**

Few researchers have collated multiple treatments, and doctors have limited information to decide which intervention is more suitable. Lanovaz et al. (2014) examine this limitation collateral effect in 12 individuals with an autism spectrum disorder to develop a sequential intervention system. His studies provide evidence of best treatment practices for treating speaking

8

stereotypy in children diagnosed with autism (Lanovaz et al., 2014). Lanovaz et al. (2014) conducted four single-case experiments that showed noncontingent music produces better outcomes than differential treatment (DRO). Differential treatment lower speaking stereotypy in conditions that noncontingent music could not treat. Adding another prompting procedure enhances the effect of interventions (Lanovaz et al., 2014). The impact of treatment with reinforcement music persists during sessions where the practitioners extend the treatment durations.

Reinforcement music is playing favorite music consistently through headphones or an external speaker. The advantage of the method is that it is the cheapest treatment for speaking stereotypy. The nurse can turn on their favorite music and attend other activities. The noncontingent music access is not disruptive to others when headphones are used. Lanovaz et al. (2014) were concerned with playing noncontingent music. It can encourage engagement in the wrong types of stereotypy; from that viewpoint, better treatment should lower vocal stereotypy and not introduce another.

Similarly, no evidence shows the method will affect the person's appropriate behavior. However, some studies suggest that soundtrack music increases recovery in children with ASD (Lanovaz et al., 2014). But another study reported mixed results, while another produced zero effect. Finally, a study on exposure to noncontingent music for five to ten seconds revealed that the student with autism might stop engaging with the item (headphones, speaker) after repeated exposure (Lanovaz et al., 2014). Hence, the method cannot continue during extended sessions, and the music play through the session regardless of the student's behavior. Similarly, the effect will differ because the student is not engaged in response to access the music in extended sessions.

9

Lanovaz et al. (2014) confirm that the differential response of alternative behavior is one of the best empirical supports for reducing vocal stereotypy. Its advantage is that DRO strengthens appropriate behavior and minimizes the probability of being replaced with another type of stereotypy (Lanovaz et al., 2014). However, most studies were conducted on motor because verbal is connected with other stereotypes.

Lanovaz et al. (2014) compared reinforcement music treatment and the different responses of another habit. They found that in two participants, one intervention reduced vocal stereotypy in up to five of the seven participants. Noncontingent music immediately reduced speaking stereotypes in other participants and encouraged engagement in proper behavior in two (Lanovaz et al., 2014). Differential responses to alternative behavior immediately reduced speaking stereotypy in other participants and encouraged proper habits in one. However, in two children, both treatments did not give the expected outcome, indicating the benefit of exploring another treatment option (Lanovaz et al., 2014). These results indicate DRO may be helping when the first treatment fails to correct the stereotypy condition and may be an appropriate method in the successive treatment model.

While providing noncontingent access to music reduces vocal stereotypy. Research indicates it might cause an untargeted type of stereotypy. Therefore Lanovaz et al. (2014) experimented with adding prompts to increase engagement in proper habits when a student with autism spectrum disorder does not engage in proper behavior. The result suggests that combining DRA with prompt reduces vocal and other forms of motor stereotypy but marginally increases face touching (Lanovaz et al., 2014). The impact of reinforcement music when a prompt is added shows a consistent reduction in instant engagement in speaking stereotypy but to a little extent than deferential treatment. Adding contingent music to DRA and prompting treat vocal stereotypy more widely (Lanovaz et al., 2014). The result ceases to produce significant post-intervention and extended exposure duration changes, indicating that prompting does not interfere with noncontingent music or DRA effectiveness.

**Conclusion**

Stereotypy is indicated by multiple topographies, including repetition of unintelligible sounds, noncontextual phrases, and echolalia. The paper is a literature review of studies and research journals aiming to treat vocal stereotypy in a child with autism condition. The experiments on reducing vocal stereotypy mainly produce varied results. Examination of the differential response of alternative habit, nonlinguistic contingent response. Imitation, linguistic contingent response, and vocal self-stimulation. Red card versus green card, contingent music, and promptly indicated combination of these methods produce recommendable results than a single intervention. The results on exposure to more extended periods were not significantly different from exposure to short intervals. Adding a prompt does not interfere with the desired result in contingent music or differential response to alternative behavior. Contingent music alone reduces vocal stereotypy but increases other forms of motor stereotypy. Prompting and contingent stereotypy was less effective than adding a prompt and differential response to alternative habit. When reinforcement music fails to reduce ASD, DRA is the best method, as research suggests exploring other better methods. Therefore adding prompts is essential in increasing appropriate behavior. The study suggests that in a sequential intervention model, practitioners should start with contingent music, then DRA, and a combined intervention with adding a prompt.

# References

Ahearn, W. H., Clark, K. M., & MacDonald, R. P. (2007). *Assessing and Treating Vocal Stereotypy in Children with Autism*. National Library of Medicine. https://www.ncbi.nlm.nih.gov/pmc/articles/PMC1885411/

Dunlop, K. A. (2012). *Reducing Vocal Stereotypy through an Antecedent and Consequence Intervention Package*. https://repository.library.northeastern.edu/files/neu:997/fulltext.pdf

Esposito, M., Pignotti, L., Mondani, F., D'Errico, M., Ricciardi, O., Mirizzi, P., Mazza, M., & Valenti, M. (2021). *Stimulus Control Procedure for Reducing Vocal Stereotypies in an Autistic Student*. National Library of Medicine. https://www.ncbi.nlm.nih.gov/pmc/articles/PMC8700641/

Kahveci, G., & Bulut, S. N. (2019). Shaping vocal stereotypy in autism spectrum disorder: a non-aversive communication teaching technique. *Universal Journal of Education Research, 7*(6), 1448-1457. https://www.hrpub.org/download/20190530/UJER12-19512777.pdf

Lanovaz, M. J., Rapp, J. T., Maciw, I., Pregent-Pelletier, E., Dorion, C., Ferguson, S., & Saade, S. (2014). The effects of multiple interventions for reducing vocal stereotypy include developing a sequential intervention model. *Elsevier*, 529-545. https://www.sciencedirect.com/science/article/pii/S1750946714000208/pdfft?md5=542ce2b2689177508c99721e292f22d5&pid=1-s2.0-S1750946714000208-main.pdf

Lanovaz, M. J., & Sladeczek, I. E. (2011). *Vocal Stereotypy in Individuals with Autism Spectrum Disorders: A Review of Behavioral Interventions*. Paneecioccolata. https://www.paneecioccolata.com/wp2/wp-content/uploads/2013/06/Lanovaz-2011-vocal-stereotipy-review.pdf

Memari, A. H., Panahi, N., Ranjbar, E., Moshayedi, P., Shafiei, M., Kordi, R., & Ziaee, V.

(2015, Jan 15). *Children with Autism Spectrum Disorder and Patterns of Participation in*

*Daily Physical and Play Activities*. Neurology Research International.

https://www.hindawi.com/journals/nri/2015/531906/

Posar, A., Corinaldesi, A., & Parmeggiani, A. (2019). Early Features of Autism Spectrum

Disorder: a Cross-Sectional Study. *Italian Journal of Pediatrics*, *45*, 144.

https://ijponline.biomedcentral.com/articles/10.1186/s13052-019-0733-8

Sălăgean, C. S., & Stan, C. N. (2020). Reducing vocal self-stimulation in children with autism

spectrum disorders. *European Proceedings*.

https://www.europeanproceedings.com/article/10.15405/epsbs.2020.06.3